Off Grid as a Single Woman - Ideal Life

How a ballet dancer left the glittering glamorous world of ballet ...

for a simple sustainable life in a magical forest off grid

MY HOME

Dedication

This book is dedicated to the beautiful Buddhist Jerry E. Aurand.

Copyright Notice

ISBN: 9798842290130

Introduction

This book was written with love, kindness, and gentleness for my many sisters around the world. It is my intention that this book should give you hope and encourage you to live the life that you most desire. Hopefully, you'll be able to use at least a few of these suggestions. I'm working on a Ph.D. in Philosophy as it relates to living an ideal life with nature. Sometimes folks are able to consistently live well, at other times, we sometimes sabotage our own values and ideals. Life isn't always easy, but yours *should be great* and it should be the life that you *most want to live.* This information is here to help and assist you to take the steps that you need so that *you* can get to where *you* want to go; for me it was off grid living as a single woman, for you it could be something totally different. The women who have gone on before us, stretching the height and breadth of the parameters that society and our American culture says what women can (and cannot) accomplish, have my highest respect. Without our mothers (and Grandmothers) going on before us and putting new thoughts on what a woman can and cannot do, I would not have been able to so easily, accomplish an intentional and ideal life. A simple, ideal life off-grid. An ideal life that I wish for you as well.

Contents

"Simplicity involves unburdening your life and living more lightly with fewer distractions that interfere with a high-quality life, as defined uniquely by each individual."

 - Linda Breen Pierce

"We need much less than we think we need."
 - Maya Angelou

"Joy is not in things, it's within us."
- Benjamin Franklin

"As I unclutter my life, I free myself to answer the callings of my soul."
- Dr. Wayne Dyer

"To be free is not merely to cast off one's chains, but to live in a way that respects and enhances the freedom of others."
 - Nelson Mandela

"Discard everything that does not spark joy."
 - Marie Kondo

I. LIVING AN AUTHENTIC LIFE

"He who is contented is rich". Lao Tzu

Would you like to live a lifestyle of more authenticity and intentionality in your daily life? Authenticity and intentionality that allows you to *live* your values daily? Values that matter to you? Values like healthy living, working from home, raising your children (along with raising the chickens and the garden), having the time to make your family's life better as well as your extended family or community? Values such as love and kindness-and the ability to live these beautiful values every day with everyone you meet or are around?

My life is free (I work part time), beautiful (in a forested area with thousands of acres of state forest on three sides), artistic (I'm able to write, paint, and do yoga), authentic (authentic for *me*, my friends from kindergarten say that I've been talking about this kind of life since I was ten years old), musical, academic (I'm halfway through a Ph.D.), and any and all things I want my life to be. I experience freedom, autonomy, independence, and *inescapable beauty* on the grandest scale on a daily basis. Freedom, autonomy, and the independence our founding fathers understood as being integral in a life *well lived.*

There are all kinds of lives that most certainly are lived, but are those lives *mostly* lived well? My experience is that our American culture is insane; everybody does what everyone else does; we watch awful television, have awful jobs, eat awful food, and then we let someone else raise our precious children. These are the best reasons as I can see, to *choose* living an intentional and ideal life (off-grid or on-grid). There's no one telling me what I can and can't do, if I want to have 100 chickens, as long as I keep them on my property, *I get to choose.*

One of my friends, living in a traditional expensive home, can't have a clothesline to dry her clothes (even though its' 100 degrees at her place in the summer), or have solar panels (the CCR's prevent that as well). The best part of living off grid is to have *the ability* to joyously embrace the freedom of living well. And nature has a lot to do with this; being in beautiful surroundings (mine have glorious snowcapped mountain peaks on one side, and salt water on the other), and seeing the glory and beauty of songbirds, red hawks, bald eagles, frogs, mule deer and Roosevelt elk every single day greatly add to the fabric-the texture and tapestry- of my life's experiences. You'll feel this way too! (Research proves that being close to nature results in greater well-being.)

There's no one way to make the move to off-grid, however what I advocate is simple, easy, and *oh-so 1950's:*

In a nutshell, this is how to do it:

1) Live below your means (your income should be greater than your debt).
2) Pay off all debt (except your mortgage-more on that later). Do not incur additional debt.
3) Save money for a down payment on property in the area you want to live off-grid.
   Where do you most want to live? If you're open to moving very far, you can check county codes as there seems to be huge variations in the size of homes allowed. There is a representative in Washington State who is trying to make it legal to build tiny homes (400 or less square feet) in cities with a population of less than 125,000 people. Portland Oregon has a tiny house movement that is the leader for the rest of the country.
4) Buy a piece of property within five years by yourself or with a close friend or member of your family. Pay for it outright or buy it from a person who is willing to carry a contract.
5) Before you make the move, have 1) passive income (i.e., a rental property to help support you, talked about further down, and/or dividends from mutual funds/stocks), 2) a day job, and 3) Instagram, a website or selling books to help support you.

6) Move. Don't worry too much about *all* of the details. You'll decide as you go what you'll want to bring with you, and what you'll want to leave behind at the Goodwill store. Give as much of your stuff away as possible; it is incredibly freeing.

7) Be prepared to live small (at least initially); there's less financial stress that way; could you borrow or rent a R.V. for a year or two while you build your cabin?

I began my quest for a life off grid while still working 60-hour weeks. I had bought (hook, line, and sinker) into the thought that in our American culture *more* was essential for my happiness (more clothes, more vacations, more stuff for my home, more new cars, etc.), and then once I achieved *more*, I was consumed with getting and buying *more* yet again. I was fed up with how I felt, how I had to give up time with my teen-age son to work yet more, and I was never (ever) content or joyful (no matter what I bought more of). As a classical ballet dancer, my body naturally was thin, and when under stress, I lost more weight. I couldn't eat enough to stay content and was stressed enough that I was always in danger of losing more weight. I was overworked, under loved, under fed, and never content (did I mention *never ever* joyful?). Something had to change.

Let me start at the beginning of my quest for a life off-grid.

BEFORE OFF-GRID, THERE WAS LIFE ON-GRID

When I was in my 30's and 40's, I ran, concurrently, two successful classical ballet studios in Washington State. Washington State is evenly divided in half; the eastern half of the state has the dry, hot desert climate (some of my cousins visiting from California used to remark that the Evergreen State certainly should **not** include Eastern Washington), with the Western half of Washington State being the lush, green forest that most folks think of when they think of Washington State and certainly Seattle. In the two beautiful ballet studio's I owned, I had twelve teachers working for me and three office staff. I was the main teacher in two studio's (80 miles apart). I had spent a lifetime in ballet; there was never a time that I didn't love what I did (except when I began to hate *the business* of ballet). As a child growing up with the best of the best of classical ballet teachers, I loved the beauty of the dance, and the way my body felt when dancing. It's a natural fact that athletes of many kinds get a high of sorts while exercising and moving their body; that's the way it generally is for ballet dancers as well.

When my son Jon was in 7th grade, he was in the Northwest division of a spelling bee with students from four western states in Portland, Oregon (about 225 miles from where we lived). Jon's spelling ability was remarkable for his age; he has somewhat of a photographic memory and because he grew up without a television, he was well read. His ability to correctly spell words allowed him to go to this Portland, Oregon championship spelling bee. I drove him to Portland, but because I had ballet rehearsals the next day for a production of Cinderella, I had to leave and miss his on-stage performance (he got 2nd place in the Northwest division that had 55 entrants). I was so angry with myself for allowing that to happen, and still fume somewhat (note to self; let peace of mind *always* be the deciding factor).

I had about 500 students in two studios; I had a growing and thriving web-site business selling marketing tools to other ballet professionals, and a few residential rental properties. I was making $125,000 a year (in the best of times), had the respect and honor that comes with the arts well done, and from all outward signs, had everything that I could possibly want. Except that no one knew how awful my life had become; work was all encompassing, my son was shifted from relative to relative based on his activities that I could get to, and every last penny was going toward making this fiasco of a ballet life great for everybody but me. Something had to give. And it did; with a sad and shaming bankruptcy.

THE BANKRUPTCY

My hardcore work ethic and my ability to juggle many plates allowed me to purchase a beautiful commercial building in Eastern Washington. Along with this commercial property, I had (as mentioned earlier) several residential rental properties. In order to buy this commercial property for one of my ballet studios', I had to place my rental properties as collateral to get a Small Business Administration (SBA) loan (just for the record, I don't *ever* recommend that anyone get an SBA loan). Then the economy changed in my community of approximately 250,000 people (I lived in a government town where about 50,000 people were employed in or at some aspect of the facilities). Well, you can imagine what happened. At the first sign of less money coming into a family, the extravagances or luxuries have to go. And ballet lessons have always been a luxury item. So, I went from making over $100,000 a year to about half of my income, which still seems like a lot, but I had all of these credit obligations to pay off. So, after a time of about a year where I tried to sell my business, tried to sell the building to other businesses, tried to work out a deal or plan with the bank so that I could pay less on the commercial building, I was eventually obligated to claim bankruptcy. And the bankruptcy turned out to be the reason for a beautiful silver lining in one of the most shaming and saddening experiences of my life. So, while I was obligated to go through the bankruptcy, I began to plan an exodus from the hellish lifestyle that the business of ballet had become, and towards an overwhelmingly better, more fulfilling, healthier, and holistic life. This was the beginning of an *intentional* life for me; an ideal life that would prove to be more loving, healthier, and more filled with my preferred community of like-minded folks.

THE LAND

My parents bought ten acres of vacation property in 1973. We used to come up as a family and camp on it. When I was fourteen years old and camping on my parent's vacation property, I thought I would die of *boredom*, nothing but trees, trees, (more trees) and rain. Incredibly boring, nothing to do but walk, hike, and eat. The ten

acres (and surrounding thousands of acres of state forest) have
majestic cedar trees (the local Native Americans have made not only
canoes out of these cedar trees, but also rainproof clothing and
impermeable roofs for their lodgings for hundreds of years),
tamarack and hemlock, but the forests are mostly filled with tall
(hundreds of feet tall), of stately Douglas fir trees. The Doug fir
lumber is some of the best in the world as it grows up straight and
tall; we're shipping these trees all around the world. So, Mom and
Dad had ten acres of land. Land without power, without water, and
a two hundred square foot cabin that by now had a leaky roof and a
rotting floor. So, when my ballet life and work became too hectic for
me to contemplate continuing, I thought of Mom and Dad's land,
and how great it would be to live there; simply, quietly, and most
importantly, peacefully-without the noise and hustle and bustle of
ordinary life working at a job that I was really dying at. My body was
rail thin (un-healthily so), my mind was filled with the jumble of what
needed to be done at work, and I had no time to call my own (none
at all; even the weekends were filled with endless ballet rehearsals,
accounting, phone calls, and all the rest of the things one must do to
survive self-employed).

The question became, then, could I live on much less income while
living an authentic, intentional, and holistic life outside of my ballet
life? How could I support myself without the work I'd always done?
So, after a few months of realizing that I was dreaming of leaving my
life's work (the only work I'd ever known), and moving across state, I
began to consider the possibilities. With my parents' blessings, and
after preparing for a year or two, saving money (small amount just to
build the shell of a 320 square foot cabin), I left for the other side of
the state, and started my latest and greatest (full-of-courage for me)
adventure as a single woman; in what I like to call my quest for an
ideal life off-grid. I lived in a small travel trailer the first summer that
I borrowed from a neighbor, while we were building my cabin. This
was the seminal beginning of *living* the good life; a life filled with
health, nature, community and so totally holistic. I was so happy that
first summer; every morning I woke up knowing that I was doing
something positive for my future. The new neighbors that I had, I
had met (most of them) when I was in my teens and 20's, and they

became the ones that I began to spend most of my time with-dining, hiking, etc. I became aware (that first summer) of just how blessed I was to have finally gotten out of the rat race that my life had become.

Every day you spend on lining another's pockets with gold (by working for and in corporate America), you're taking away the time that you could be spending working to benefit your own family. The only time I can see where working for a corporation would be beneficial would be when making money enough so that you are effectively paying off your debt and saving money to build a small, reasonable home to live in. While working for another, it could be wise to start your own business, without borrowing money, and figure out the kinks while you're still working and receiving an income from your regular day job.

Speaking of small, reasonable homes; living off grid does not usually allow one to easily build and live in a modern 2500 square foot home. Most off-grid homes are reasonable and well, *small.* Perhaps not as small as mine (320 square feet), but all of my off-grid neighbors have homes that are 800 square feet to 1500 square feet. The smallest homes are cheaper to build, easier to build, and one is able to put in extra beautiful fixtures because there simply aren't so many places to put the extra beautiful features in!

After building my small home a few years ago, I'm still not through with the building process. I don't have siding on ½ of my cabin, I've only recently dug a well (300 feet down), and had a small bathroom installed.

Don't let not having everything done stop you from living the life you want! Make do with an outhouse (mine is exceptionally beautiful; a glass roof overhead where I can see the trees dance in the wind and see the rain splatter on the roof) and be okay taking outdoor showers. Outdoor showers are so nice! The sun is shining on one's body while feeling the warm shower water course down your skin; exquisite! Our neighbor, the guru Jerry rigged up a five-gallon watering can that I partially filled with boiling water and then filled up the rest of the way with rainwater and then used a pulley system to manage my shower with. It also helped to have the cabin warm and toasty with a fire going, so that I could run in and dry off. I can't tell you how sensuous and real that outdoor shower was for me. It would be for you too! I did have to have water delivered to my place every other week for the first five years. Don't let not having water stop you! You can wash with rainwater and use the water that you're having delivered (or you can haul it yourself) for drinking and cooking. I used a three-gallon beautiful glass beverage container that ladies use for outdoor parties. I had this beverage container on a secure kitchen windowsill-right over my sink. I would use that water to fill up my pots for any cooking I was doing. Every morning I would re-fill the beverage container with more water, bring additional wood from the woodshed outside into the wood chest inside, as well as any of the other normal things one does daily like vacuuming, doing dishes, sweeping, and preparing food. We can get by on much less money and more simply, than what we think! And it's so organic and holistic; the ability to tie into nature, live simply (easily and without stress), and with beauty around you is……. everything beautiful and sublime.

Before you buy property to live on, consider paying off all of your debts, and then purchasing rental property. Working from this viewpoint, I'll let you know what worked for me (I bought rental property-talked about further down)! It could be prudent for you to work for several years to simply set yourself up with income so as to augment your lifestyle once you're living where you want to be. Once you're ready to begin looking for property to live on, consider not only the internet in the area you want, but also their local newspapers. Local newspapers have classified ads that older folks would still use in advertising their property. And you could also put your own ad in. I've heard of folks putting ads in the local newspaper asking to buy one to ten acres from someone willing to sell. And these same folks have found sellers willing to carry a contract with a large down payment. Land can be purchased away from the cities for as little as $50,000 dollars with a $20,000 down payment. This could be you! Let the work begin! Pay off your debt, buy a rental property, and then purchase land! Other folks have done it, so can you!

THE CABIN

My cabin has a footprint of 320 square feet (20 feet by 16 feet) with a sleeping loft upstairs. I had a logger clear about one acre of my forest and decided to build my home with a southern exposure (that was a good decision, as in the wintertime sunlight pours through all of the glass windows the entire length of the day). Three sides of the cabin (East, South, and West) are all glass windows. The front doors (eight foot tall by three feet wide) are two big beautiful, beveled glass doors. Jim, the neighborhood construction guy, laughed and said that he built this cabin to accommodate those doors! Yes! (I also have stained glass windows on two sides of the cabin as I had bought and saved windows specifically for the cabin I wanted-my chicken coop has stained glass windows too!) To make my cabin a home, I have *very few pieces* of beautiful furniture, my grandmothers large painting of a white knight on a horse, my mother's beautiful china, and flowers and plants blooming everywhere. Bird feeders are outside and amuse me and my family all year long with their silly antics (our hummingbirds are little kamikaze guys-attacking and then relenting-eating and then beginning the attack yet again). Some of the birds that like to eat at my place daily are:

Nuttall's Woodpecker,

Chestnut Backed Chickadee,

Warblers,

Sparrows,

Dark-Eyed Juncos,

Black-Headed Grosbeak,

and Evening Grosbeak.

Lovely! All day long the birds come to the various feeders around the windows and sing and eat (except for the hummingbirds who eat and attack). All beautiful, real, and rewarding. I feel that this is what life is about. Life and love in its simplest and earthiest forms. When did our culture lose the ability to live like this the majority of time? Who amongst us has had the great fortune to *grow up* like this? Can you change your family dynamics to begin a brand-new legacy or heritage that is simply *better* than the one you grew up in? One permeated with more warmth, greater love, and being able to assimilate a healthy life outdoors?

I have a seasonal pond outside my front door; when the rains begin in our part of Washington State in October, and the water begins its' earthly descent (almost daily for the next six months), a beautiful, watery addition to my meadow forms. In the springtime thousands and thousands of tiny frogs come to life and keep a chorus of their gentle croaking going morning, noon, and

night. Their deep-throated singing begins with just a frog or two, and then is joined in by their brethren. The magic comes, however, when all of a sudden 30 minutes later, they just stop. Period. No winding down, no big voice letting the others know, they all just stop. Incredible. And then, after a short time, they begin again…. lovely!

Just about the time that the frogs quit singing, the wild ducks begin to fly into the pond to prepare themselves for laying eggs and nearby nesting.

The ducks are a persnickety bunch; evidently, they don't like newcomers and come only in groups that swim together; when a newcomer comes to the pond, one or two of the others (both the hens and drakes) will swim and chase after the newcomer until he gets the drift and will leave and fly away towards a friendlier pond. Amusing and so enjoyable to see.   Some dogs might chase ducks, but my own dogs prefer to not chase ducks. My big girl dog (Great Pyrenees, 130 pounds) doesn't much like crows; she's seen too many of them steal her food; thus the crows, not the ducks, have become her mortal enemy. I have a crow "fly-by"; an area of my property that the crows and ravens use daily during their routine flights. These crows and ravens have big, humongous wings that one can hear 30 feet under them-they go *whoosh, whoosh, whoosh*, as they make their way to the other side of the property. Sometimes they'll "caw, caw, caw" and wait for a response from one of their buddies; those crows and ravens have a lot to say to one another!

THE FIRST FIVE YEARS

"The wisdom of life consists in the elimination of non-essentials". Lin Yutang.

As I said earlier, I lived in an eight foot by sixteen-foot travel trailer for four months while my cabin was being built. I was so excited to get out of the rat race that my life had become, that I would've been willing to live in a tent! The shell of the cabin was ready for me to move into at the end of September. I had lived in the travel trailer until the weather was just beginning to turn cool; I was now just in time to move into the cabin and enjoy the wood stove. The upstairs sleeping loft was undone; no insulation, no finished inside walls or ceiling completed-just the closed in roof. Today, I usually close the sleeping loft off during the day, and open up the hatch at night so as to save the heat for downstairs.

Not only did I have a glass front wood-stove but had also purchased a used under the counter propane refrigerator and apartment sized small propane oven/stove. I keep the bare essentials in the refrigerator, and store eggs, cheese, wine, and butter in the "cold storage". A cold storage is essential for off-grid and small living as it enables one to keep perishables cool without a huge refrigerator. Cold storages used to be common in kitchens before the 1930's but are now out of date (unless you happen to live with a small refrigerator!). Cold storages are usually insulated food lockers vented on the North side of your home. Mine works perfectly. I keep most of my vegetables and fruits in there as well.

Could you do with a stove and refrigerator that is smaller than what you're using now? My 19" stove is considered an "apartment stove", but it cooks a 20-pound turkey and two pies in it! What more does one need? I have to admit that while living off grid I sometimes *do* miss cooking with a crock-pot. I do have electricity, but things like an iron, blow-dryer, and crock pot use more electricity than what my system can easily handle. So, my answer is to use a heavy-duty cast iron Dutch oven and cook my food on top of my wood stove for eight hours. I like the idea of free anything; anytime I don't have to pay for food, or electricity, or water, I consider that great, great, GREAT! So, as long as I am using wood to heat my home with, I'd just as soon cook on it as well. Perhaps this will be as you'll think too. I think that our culture is about as wasteful as it can possibly be; we have dishes for this, and dishes for that (pans to bake fish in, pans to bake cakes in, pans to bake bread in, etc.), how about consolidating and using one or two pans for everything you need? I discovered that I could cook a 20-pound turkey in my eight-quart pot by draping tin foil around the top of the bird so that the juice would flow back into the pot. I'm adamantly opposed to buying those throw-away containers for a single use; I'd rather use and make do with what I already have.

The first four years off grid, I worked part time, about 30 hours a week. The fifth year, I took a job on the other side of the state (lasted about a year) that allowed me to save a great deal of money and drill a $16,000 well. That year was a beautiful one for me in many respects; I stayed with a friend and was able to make money enough to buy what I needed to finish my cabin.

THE EQUIPMENT YOU NEED

Living off grid does require certain components: solar panels, an inverter, generator, batteries, woodstove, propane refrigerator and stove, and the wonderful cold storage.

SOLAR PANELS

INVERTER

GENERATOR

I bought an Onan generator from Costco eight years ago for $1,600.
A good generator is money well spent. The best kind of generator is
probably a Honda; they go on working for a lifetime and can also use

the same propane gas that you'll want to use for your refrigerator
and stove. You can't expect an off-grid lifestyle to support an
electric refrigerator or stove. Propane refrigerators and stoves cost
more than electric refrigerators and stoves. You'll simply have to
spend more money to purchase a propane stove and refrigerator.
My refrigerator is small and is an under the counter one that I bought
used. Because I don't have many processed foods, this is big enough
for me. The only problem with an under the counter refrigerator is
that the freezer is not big enough to hold ice cream; awful for me
who loves to eat ice cream! I also can't freeze much meat or have
ice cubes in there either. I've learned to do without-and it's saved
me a bundle over the years on propane costs. Propane for a small
stove and refrigerator costs me about $50.00 a month. I do have to
spend money on gasoline for my Oman generator (about $20.00 a
month), but the savings on my monthly bills in general is HUGE.
The cost savings you'll have each month will be huge as well. This is
another reason to enjoy a simple life off-grid; it simply costs less
(once you've bought what you need)!

BATTERIES

My first batteries were those that cars use. When I upgraded a few
years ago, I went to golf cart batteries for my needs. A better battery
than that, even, would be marine batteries. Batteries are essential in
order to use electricity in the evening when the sun isn't out. The
battery stores the energy from the solar panels and is utilized as
regular electricity with the use of an inverter.

WOODSTOVE

I have a "Regency" woodstove that I bought used. It has a glass
front, and easily heats a small cabin. The folks selling it had bought it
new and never used it. I got a top-notch great woodstove for $600.
A good woodstove is essential for your comfort. It could be a good
idea to get something that you could cook on easily. In the
wintertime you may have your woodstove going 20 hours a day-it's
nice then, to be able to utilize that free heat to cook with. I don't
recommend pellet stoves for heat, as you don't want to be

dependent upon having to buy anything you don't absolutely need (and you can always cut your own wood).

PROPANE REFRIGERATOR AND OVEN

My refrigerator and oven are small. My refrigerator is an under the counter one that I bought used, now that I'm thinking about it, my oven was bought used as well. Because I don't have many processed foods, the refrigerator is big enough for me.

COLD STORAGE

Building and using a cold storage is….so…. beautiful, not the least of which is that the ability to use it costs absolutely nothing! A cold storage can be built into your cabin and vented on the north side (so it stays cool most of the year). As stated earlier, my cold storage keeps all of my vegetables, eggs, and some cheeses cool most of the year. In the heat of late summer, for a month or two, the cold storage doesn't stay cold enough (where I live in the Pacific Northwest), so I simply buy fewer vegetables and cheese then. I do shop in a local organic market most every week, so it's not an issue to keep a week's worth of vegetables in the cold storage. I have also, just in the last few months, made a second cold storage holding area on the North side of my cabin.

II. HOW TO GET TO WHERE YOU WANT TO BE: FINANCING YOUR LIFE

"Be content with what you have; rejoice in the way things are. When you realize there is nothing lacking, the whole world belongs to you". Lao Tzu.

OK, now we're getting to the part that I'm super excited about…. how you're going to make it happen. First, you'll need to pay off your debt. You'll need to get rid of your credit card bills, your car payments, and anything else you have bought on credit (I've lived that life too; once you get out of it, you'll realize how ridiculous living that way is). You need to think that your life will be one with zero credit card payments, zero car payments, if you have a house in the city that you're paying off, that's ok, don't worry about paying that off, assuming you can turn it into a rental; and this is where I'm going to talk you into buying rental property while you're still working a day job and saving money for a piece of off-grid property. To live a great life takes time to get to where you need to be; this could be a two-year (or longer) venture. Be aware that you can indeed do anything if you set your mind to it. A year (or two or three) to pay off bills is way better than continuing to rack up debt. You can do this! Other folks have spent a few years paying off bills, you can too! Create the circumstances you need around you in order to be able to do this; your day job (plus maybe a second job), living below your means, and trimming your regular monthly bills. You can do this!

PAYING OFF YOUR DEBT

There are so many fantastic books on this particular subject, but in a nutshell, this is how it's done:

1) List everything you owe money on (car, home, credit cards, student loans, etc.), who you owe money to, how much you pay each month, and the overall amounts owed.
2) List all of the sources of income that you have (day job, passive income, dividends, bonuses from work, real estate rentals, etc.), and the amounts you receive each month.

3) List everything else that you spend money on each month (i.e., groceries, gas, gym membership, cell phone, restaurants, etc.)

4) Hopefully, you're bringing in more money per month than spending. THIS IS WHERE YOU ABSOLUTELY MUST BE (if not already). YOU MUST BE BRINGING IN MORE MONEY PER MONTH THAN YOU'RE SPENDING.

   A) Assuming that you are bringing in more money than you're spending each month, list your bills from highest amount owed to lowest amount owed; here's an example- Credit Card A $9500 owed, Credit Card B $6000 owed, Credit Card C $1500 owed. (Don't put in your mortgage payments or car payments in this particular assignment.) Pay the minimum monthly amount on Credit Card A, the minimum monthly amount on Credit Card B, and **pay as much as you can** on Credit Card C. Once you're through paying off Credit Card C, take what you were paying on Credit Card C, and begin to pay off Credit Card B, while still paying the minimum on Credit Card A.) At the end of each payoff, celebrate with something that matters to you!

5) So, the whole situation, here, is to pay off your debts as quickly as possible. Here are a few ways to pay off debt (by raising income and lowering payments on essential monthly fees):

   A) Call 5 insurance agents and see about lowering your mortgage and car insurance. Consider having a higher deductible ($5000) on your home so you'll have a lower monthly payment on your home insurance.

   B) Consider getting rid of your car that you're making payments on and buy a used car.

   C) Quit buying. Period. Don't buy yourself clothes, vacations, jewelry. Don't buy birthday presents, Christmas presents, anniversary presents, or anything that requires cash. Make a beautiful homemade card, give your possessions away as gifts, or give your friends and lover a great homemade picnic lunch with a 3-hour hike. Every part of your life that you're spending money on should be suspect; quit spending money. Quit spending money *now*. Don't go to restaurants *except* rarely and then only for special occasions. That being said, life is meant to be enjoyed! My Mother used to say that life is too short to be unhappy. Live your life well! But maybe not like how everybody else is living….be aware that each time you spend money on something other than towards the life you *really* want, you'll be putting up roadblocks on your path…. don't let that happen to you. Do the goal setting exercise (coming up) and begin your quest towards living your values.

D) Move to someplace less expensive. Or get a roommate. Or become a roommate. Your job is to consider every single aspect of your life (and your expenses) as potential money-drains; fix the problems. Fix the problems *now*. Don't continue to live as you've always lived, unless you want what you're always getting….and you're way too smart for that….

E) Get a second job. You won't need to work a second job forever, but how about for right now, this particular season? You could use this second job to get out of debt.

F) Re-think every aspect of how you spend money: Could you enjoy picnics outside at a beautiful park instead of going out to eat? Could you enjoy (even moderately) hiking in the nearby woods instead of spending money on a gym membership? Or at least walking for an hour in your neighborhood each evening instead of spending money on a gym membership (or watching the soul-sucking boob tube)?

SAVING MONEY

"The secret of happiness is not found in seeking more, but in developing the capacity to enjoy less". Socrates.

Go through all of your weekly, monthly, and yearly expenses. Some of these expenses may be:

1) Insurance (car, home, renters, boat, rental property, health, long-term care)
2) Food (from the grocery store)
3) Eating food out
4) Products (make-up, toilet paper, shampoo, cleaning products)
5) Clothes
6) Animal/pet care
7) Internet/television
8) Cell phones
9) Rent or mortgage payments

At this time, you should have everything written down; how much you're spending on your life. The point of this particular exercise (or eye opener) is to simply be aware of how much money you're spending. Call five different insurance carriers and giving them the same data, you're currently spending your money on, compare the apples you're paying for with the apples this other insurance company can give you. For years I continued to pay the insurance company that I had been with for years and years. When I did this one simple exercise (and called several insurance carriers to compare what I was currently spending vs. what they were able to give me) for my own insurance needs, I saved $400.00 a month! As much as I appreciated my local insurance folks, I would rather pay myself $400 a month so that I could work less and live life more…perhaps you'll feel the same? Something you may want to consider is to have a higher deductible (both for your car and your home), which would give you a lower monthly insurance fee. Or, alternatively, get rid of the car you're making payments on (with a high insurance fee), and get an older, less expensive car (pay for outright), and have lower insurance payments on that too.

OWNING RENTAL PROPERTY

The reason to own real estate is to essentially own an *income-producing* asset (unlike cars, or the homes we live in, or 401K's). An income producing asset produces income…. *for you* every single month, rain or shine. Sometimes initially, only a little and then later on a lot! (A gal who subscribes to this theory first bought a rental property-a four-unit small apartment building-, and received $200 a month positive cash flow, now fifteen years later, she's bringing in $2100 a month positive cash flow because of rent increases), and all the while the equity in her place keeps increasing. To own a piece of rental income is scary…. most folks don't own rental property because they've heard so many horror stories of being a landlord. Yes, it can be scary to own rental property just for that fact; tenants can bring drugs into your place, have wild parties until four in the morning and the cops have to be called, bad tenants can bash holes in your walls, and tear down your light fixtures. But those are the worst-case scenarios….

The reality is that you will have policies in place to prevent tenant nightmares. All of your tenants will have a day job, will have no credit problems in their credit reports, and will pay you on time (except for the occasional time when a car breaks down, a family health crisis, etc., all of these can be handled graciously and easily by you). When I am ready to rent one of my places, I utilize a background and credit screening agency (there are lots available on the internet). My credit screening agency is called Rent Prep. Rent Prep needs social security numbers, and a signed affidavit that the prospective tenant signs to agree for me to run a background and credit check on them. Its cost is about $40 per person. I used it recently and discovered that the couple that wanted to rent both had bad credit histories; bad credit histories are not OK, we only want to rent to people who are used to paying their bills. Owning rental property is great, it's do-able, manageable, and owning rental property is a perfect vehicle *specifically* for the passive income flow it'll generate for you to live off grid with. Many folks who live off-grid have relied on rental property to augment their own intentional life.

BUYING RENTAL PROPERTY

The ability to buy a piece of real estate and have it work for you is *to buy right.* This means (in a perfect world) to buy it undervalued. A lady I know bought an 1100 square foot foreclosed house with a 400 square foot mother-in-law cottage on it in 2014. They had to take out a $25,000 construction loan to get both homes up to code, but then the two homes appraised at $135,000. The homes in 2021 appraised at $330,000. I call that buying a great piece of property! You can do this too!

Smart folks buy rental property for three main reasons: 1) cash flow, 2) appreciation on the property, and 3) the deductions available. If you are able to purchase a duplex to live in for a year or so, you are in the **best** of situations. You'll be able to buy it via an FHA or a Conventional mortgage. FHA and Conventional mortgages are made available through your local bank, credit union, Costco, and other mortgage companies online. You may want to contact five local credit unions and banks to find out who will allow you to purchase a duplex to live in, as some banks won't give a mortgage to anything other than a single-family home without a conventional loan. You'll also want to purchase your new rental with (preferably) 20% down of the purchase price. This will mean that you'll be obligated to save money for a while, but this is important! This is *so much more* important than buying a new fancy car like a Porsche! Fancy new cars are good, but not when having it prevents you from living how you really want to live. (It seems that everyone wants to own a fancy Porsche; but not me, what I *really* want to do is be invisible and fly!)

Nevertheless, save money you must! IF you put down 3.5% of the purchase price (rather than 20%), you'll be obligated to purchase mortgage insurance premium (MIP) for the life of the loan (30 years). No matter how much you want to move off-grid, and own rental property, don't allow yourself to lose $75.00 a month, every year, for 30 years; save money ahead of time so you won't be out $900.00 a year, $9000 for the first 10 years, and $27,000 over a 30-year period by having to pay the MIP. You want to own smart, not foolish! That being said, I have known folks who have been gifted half of the down payment (10%) and asked their sister to take out an additional 10% loan that they've paid back over 5-10 years. Perhaps you're lucky enough to know folks who will help you out like this!

If you have enough cash for the initial outlay, you can also buy non-owner-occupied property. This typically has a higher interest rate and may require more of a down payment (25%). Situations change from season to season, so check your local mortgage markets first.

There are real estate investment clubs that are available to join; this would be a good idea for you to do. Simply go to www.meetup.com, type in your geographical area, and put in "real estate club". Depending on the size of your community, there should be lots to choose from. Once you join, you'll get an idea of what the advantages and disadvantages are of real estate investing and the avenues to choose to go down.

There are tons of books with information on how to be a landlord; read a variety of real estate books on this first, start going through the websites that list properties available for sale, and then once you have a good chunk of money saved (20%), find a real estate agent you can connect with.

III. WHAT YOUR LIFE WILL BE LIKE OFF GRID.

WHAT TO DO ONCE YOU'RE THERE (and what to expect) IN YOUR NEW LIFE OFF GRID

Expect to feel good; really, *really good*. You'll feel good and well rested when you wake up in the morning and see and hear the beautiful songbirds right outside your window. You'll feel good and hungry at lunchtime and enjoy a healthy lunch (and, perhaps, a small siesta), and you'll still feel great at the end of the day. You'll be active during the day (I usually hike most days with friends to a lake several miles away), you'll be carrying firewood, cleaning, building and creating projects, cooking great food, and if you're extra blessed- you'll be dining in the evenings with the folks you love most in the world.   And THEN (as if life couldn't possibly get any better), you'll get to sleep for 8 hours (or more) in a soft bed with a down comforter and down pillows. At night you won't hear the sirens and horns of the city, nor will the lights of the city keep you awake; you won't be tossing and turning stressing about what you've got to accomplish at your corporate job tomorrow……however, what you *will hear* will be the frogs and crickets and coyotes doing their nighttime singing; singing their glorious nighttime songs as they've done since time immemorial. The coyotes singing with their *yip, yip, yipping* filling the gloaming of the evening and night sky with their own sweetly sublime songs.

Link to coyote songs: https://bit.ly/CoyoteSongs *

It feels *nice* to be sleeping at night with the sounds of the country being as they always have been, and what your forefathers heard as well. When you go outside at night, the stars in their exquisite glory will shine on you; softly and serenely. You'll spend whole evenings outside looking at the stars, the constellations, and marveling at the bright Milky Way. Marveling at the bright starry, starry nights like all of our forefathers did. I quite often feel connected to my grandparents (who emigrated here from Finland), knowing that they experienced country life as I do now. My grandparents were happy and healthy folks who raised six loving children (of whom I am lucky enough to call one of those children my mom). It makes me feel so *doggone good* to have that connection with the folks who have made my life possible (and who I got my adventuresome and pioneering spirit from).

A wood stove or fireplace is essential! Having fires in the fireplace or wood stove is just so cotton-pickin' cozy! We live in the Pacific Northwest where it's chilly most of the year; we have fires 9 months out of the year. It is deep-down soul satisfying to hunker down in front of the fireplace with a glass of wine, after a beautiful dinner, and have good conversation with your most favorite people! I love, love, LOVE my glass front woodstove. Not only does it put out delightful warmth, but it also shows my wood fire and the orange and yellow flames flicker throughout our small cabin-it's one of the most beautiful experiences……

I quite oftentimes cook on my woodstove; usually soups and stews that can cook most of the day (just in time for the dinner party that night). I will also, in the morning, put a slice of homemade bread to toast on the stove; it just feels so natural and right to utilize a wood stove for cooking as well as for heat. And many days have been spent inside next to a wood stove reading, while the rain is coming down in great droves outside. Listening to the rain outside sounds almost like a symphony; sometimes the rain comes down hard and strong, and then after a bit it may lighten up and merely put in a small pat-pat-patter. Being able to read a lovely book while my favorite cat is sleeping on my lap is so…. beautiful. You'll feel this way too! Listening to the rain is another aspect of beauty in my life…. when I was designing my cabin, because I love hearing and seeing the rain so much, I put huge glass skylights (that I bought used) over my bed. Sometimes the rain comes down so hard that it wakes me up and I……love……. this so much. I simply love the rain.

Some folks off-grid have television; many do not. It is my own suggestion that all folks wanting to live a healthy, intentional life should do away with their television-it simply becomes an all-consuming soul-sucking appliance. We end up living vicariously through the television shows we watch; when the reality is that we should be *living* our life. When I became interested in extreme health and living an intentional life, I got rid of our television. That was a big, huge statement into living life well *for me and my family.* I've never regretted it. Now, we can plant ourselves in front of the television and be entertained 24 hours a day. That being said, I do (sadly), have forays into major television watching.......

I am very aware when I visit friends and turn the television on (in the bedroom I've been given) in the middle of the night, how very adept the television marketers are; one week while visiting family in Portland Oregon, I ended up buying something that the late-night advertisers were selling-4 nights in a row! *4 nights in a row*! I just had to *have* those products/books/jewels/makeup! Wow! What a crazy week of television watching that was for me! Many friends I know always have their television on-and not on edifying, or uplifting channels. Garbage in-garbage out! If one were to read (for edification and growth) rather than watch television, we could, then, very well become the wise folks that some of us knew as kids…. it's up to you. You don't have to live like everyone else-what's important in your life? I encourage you to take a stand in your life; if you give up television and then *miss* having television you can always go back to it, but perhaps you would like to try (what some folks term) a *better way of living.*

Food: you're gonna love food way more than you do now. YAHOO! Food, glorious food! You'll probably take the time to cook healthier food that feeds your body (and soul) better and more soundly. In my neighborhood we make an entire evening of cooking and eating together; and usually with wine or Elaine's 'worlds' best margaritas'. We spend our evenings telling stories and laughing, laughing a lot! Friends feel better and enjoy being together when the stress level is non-existent, and life is lived intentionally. Laughing! Yes! On summer (and winter) evenings we may dine and drink outside by the bonfire only coming in to refill our drinks or to begin one of our homemade desserts. We dine by candlelight and have fires most every day, and every day is a celebration into living life well; living a life *worth* living; simply, intentionally, and authentically. Like what you'll be doing too. Your body is going to become leaner, stronger, and more able to handle the natural work you'll be doing. You'll go to sleep tired every night and wake up refreshed every morning. Your life will become more of one that is organic and holistic. Intentional. It feels really, *really* nice.

Our neighborhood guru Jerry (who once sat at the feet of and listened to the wisdom of Osho), believes in the old adage of chopping firewood and carrying water, and this is one of his main occupations during the day. That being said, he does, however, begin his work at 11:00 a.m. and quits at 3:00 p.m. Being an older gentleman, this works very well for him. You, however, may want to begin your work at 8:00 a.m. and quit at 5:00 p.m.; but however you do it, make sure you don't overwork yourself, and you must have pleasurable activities as well. Do you sing? Make crafts? Do you enjoy reading? Are there hobbies or crafts that you used to do that you *wish* you had time for again? Or hobbies and crafts that you've always wanted to make time for?

One of the crafts I used to do when I was a teenager was knitting. My mother taught me how to knit, so I decided I would re-learn knitting and make my father a scarf. Here is the sad result of this:

And then, when I discovered I couldn't knit well, I decided that as long as I wasn't a knitter, I would learn to crochet; and would crochet my father a scarf to give him the next Christmas as a present. Sadly, here is the result of this one as well!

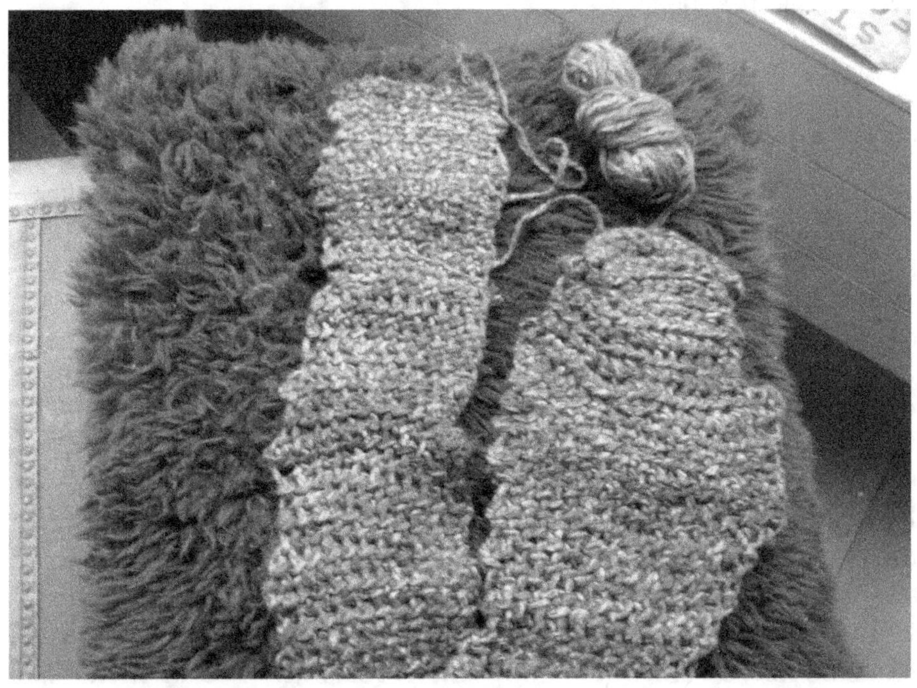

My friend Judie begged me not to give it to my dad! I so sucked at this!

One of our neighbors (a Vietnam Vet) has gotten back into his old craft of making nightlight fairy houses out of driftwood and sea glass (some of his sea glass was found in Spain in front of the famous painter of the 1930's Salvador Dali's seaside home-we all imagine that Dali and his buddies must've been sitting outside discussing (or perhaps arguing) the pros and cons of Spanish art while drinking; and would then throw the wine bottles far, far out into the ocean to break up and become the sea glass that we found 70 years later). The fairy houses are beautiful, intricate, and are made with oceans and oceans of love. This beautiful man gives these delicate fairy houses to children that he knows "because they make the children so happy", he says. The gift of these fairy houses to young children is priceless because of the work involved, and is even more valued by the young owners themselves because of the uniqueness of the art. Could this be you? Would you like to do something that matters to you? Something that really, really matters *to you?* What would that be? What could that be?

For our neighbor the Veteran, making beautiful works of art and giving them to children greatly matters, for the resident guru Jerry, being of service to others in the neighborhood (and greater community) greatly matters. For me, it's helping others find their ideal life. While in graduate school I was obligated to take a personality test and discovered that I am 3% of the population that is known to encourage others and to help elevate them-a factor in my character that I've had since I was little.

An ideal life is not what our American culture teaches; our American culture teaches that we need to keep up with the Joneses and to be uber consumers. Does consumption in any facet make you happy? Does it make anyone you know *really* happy? Did you know that the ancient sages of yore (Plato, Aristotle) advocated spending energy on relationships with people who matter? What matters to you-people or things? Meditate and write down how you would like life to be for you and your family. Many folks who live an intentional life off grid home school their children as well. Would this be wonderful for you to do too?

When I retired from ballet and moved to the country, I decided to go back to school. After spending a lifetime in the arts, I was pleased to discover that I was indeed able to pursue, grow and develop in ways that are most agreeable to me. In the last eight years, I've easily navigated an undergraduate degree (humanities), a graduate degree (adult education), and I am now halfway through a Ph.D. (philosophy). Every day I'm able to spend time reading and researching that which makes me most happy; how to self-actualize and live an ideal life (Maslow's hierarchy of needs lists self-actualization and self-transcendence as the highest of an ideal life). What would be awesome for you to spend time on that which you're not doing now? Write down 10 things now without rationalizing any part of it:

1)

2)

3)

4)

5)

6)

7)

8)

9)

10)

STRESS

At one time or another, we all are under stress: stress from our jobs, our relationships, finances, etc. So, the questions then become:

1)   Do you take better care of others than you do yourself?
2)   Do you try to do it all even when it isn't realistic?
3)   Do you ignore or downplay your own feelings or health concerns?
4)   Do you have a hard time saying "no"?
5)   Is it difficult for you to ask for help?
6)   Is finding time for yourself something you will do tomorrow?

Right now, list your stresses-the things you don't like about your life. Anxiety producing stress could begin when your children are sick, when you don't have enough money to pay the bills, when your relationships are not harmonious-go ahead and list them.

1)_________________________

2)_________________________

3)_________________________

4)_________________________

5)_________________________

Warning signs of stress:

Physical: muscle tension, stiff neck or back pain, cold/sweaty hands, tired all of the time, tension headaches, indigestion or diarrhea, high blood pressure or chest pain, ulcers, rapid heart rate, grinding of teeth.

Emotional/mental: feelings of guilt, anxiety or fear, impatience, nervousness, mood swings, short tempered or panic.

Behavioral: changes in eating or sleeping patterns, forgetfulness, having a hard time making a decision, with drawing from former activities or spending less time with friends, problems with relationships (marriage, friends, children), and the inability to rest or relax.

Now, I'd like for you to think about the things that you do (or should do) to take very good care of you. List 10 things that you can or should do to take good care of you. For myself, it's almost embarrassingly basic: I like sleep. 10 hours or more in bed is great for me. A second one is that I want good food (healthy, foods I like); I sometimes eat processed food, but for the most part I eat foods in their natural state (and I am so boring); I eat a lot of rice, potatoes, legumes, fresh and in season vegetables and fruits, organic meats. A third way that I take very good care of me is with exercise; I walk or hike most days for an hour or two, plus I do some calisthenics (I am against spending money on exercise when we have the beautiful wide world to explore and enjoy), that being said, however, I do attend a yoga class regularly as well. The fourth item for me would be in continuous learning; I love being in a Ph.D. program and the challenges it brings me. A fifth item would be great and harmonious relationships in every situation; with the family I see, my good friends, and even my casual friends-we all have harmonious and peaceful relationships. A sixth item is that of pleasant diversions; I love musicals and go into Seattle often to see my favorite ones. I also like seeing the bands I grew up with (but I don't like crowds, so I prefer to see my favorite bands in smaller venues). I just recently put in an indoor shower, so I would have to say that my seventh item in taking very good care of me would be that of showering indoors in the winter. It was difficult to take showers outside in the winter. An eighth item for me would have the ability to decorate as I see fit; my little cottage is beautiful. I had the walls painted a distressed white, I have tall ceilings, mirrors on one side of the living room, and a few beautiful antiques (a 200-year-old sleigh bed with an incredibly comfy mattress, down pillows and comforter, and topped with a lovely thick wool blanket I bought in Iceland last year). My chest of drawers in my bedroom matches the sleigh bed and came with my uncle's family when they emigrated from Italy at the turn of the 20th century. My ninth item is growing into self-actualization (becoming the best I can become), with my tenth item is becoming self-transcendent (the ability to help others grow into their ideal selves through encouragement, guidance, etc.). What are your ten items that you need to take very good care of you?

1) ____
2) ____
3) ____
4) ____
5) ____
6) ____
7) ____
8) ____
9) ____
10) ____

SIMPLE PLEASURES

Reading: I don't read many books that are fiction, most of my reading is non-fiction that I can grow from. These are some of the books that were recommended to me to help me grow, perhaps these will help you too!

7 Habits of highly effective people by Stephen Covey (1990). This is wonderful as Covey suggests that we are able to accomplish anything we want if we simply give it the recognition and due diligence it deserves to accomplish.

Your money or your life by Vicky Robins (2018). This is a real kick in the pants as this wise gal demonstrates that one can live an ideal life with passive income coming in merely by concentrating on where our money is going. This is great as most of us spend our money as fast as we can get it. Robins writes down what really matters, and how to get to where you want to be; she further states that anyone with a reasonable (not big) income can accomplish what she herself did as well.

The four agreements by Miguel Ruiz (1997). The four agreements are:

1) Don't take anything personally
2) Don't make assumptions
3) Always do your best
4) Be impeccable with your word

Dave Ramsey's website Financial Peace University. Dave Ramsey has good information in an easy-to-understand format as to how best to:

1) pay down credit cards, and
2) how (and ways) to save money
3) how to have a financial future

Ramsey suggests that one should live way below their means today, so that they can live super-duper well tomorrow (next year/next decade). This resonates with me, as there is no way that we (as a culture) can continue to spend money we don't have, buying stuff that we don't need and that we will *never* keep. Ramsey offers an eight-week class (one night weekly for eight weeks) held in churches in every single city in the country. The name of this is called *Peace University*, you can look up Dave Ramsey and *Peace University* online to see where it's offered in your particular community. Cost used to be $100 per couple. This is a beautiful class to take to adapt to simply spending less money on stuff that doesn't matter.

How about getting rid of 90% of your clothing and keep only the clothing (and shoes, coats, sweaters, etc.) that will wear well for the next 30 years? Why do we Americans think that we have to buy new so often? Can we repair the socks that have worn out? Repair the jeans that have ripped? How much money would we save if we simply quit being consumers? A lovely woman I know, Linda and her husband Don, have decided that the beginning of this new year was the year that they would **not buy anything new**. Nothing. Nada. No new shoes, boots, clothing, or even underwear. Anything they need, they've planned to buy used or simply do without. What can you do without? Can you do without that fancy fish pan you've been hankering for? Without that fancy gadget you desire for the kitchen? When do we, as a nation and culture, realize that buying more stuff won't make us any happier, and it will certainly create hardship by taking us further away from our goals, *but only if we're aware* of where our money is being spent? (As a confession, I'll admit that I love dresses; living in the forest I almost never wear dresses, but boy oh boy do I love them…. I succumbed a few months ago into buying a beautiful knee length fancy evening dress substantially on sale….and wear it now with cowboy boots and my cowboy hat).

Hiking: Health is super important. I like to hike (but not as much as I did when I was younger). Some beautiful hikes we've done around the world are:

The Cinque Terre in Italy.

This is a series of five picturesque villages that used to be connected with only a goat trail between them on the Mediterranean. In the olden days, folks would have to come into the villages via the ocean, on the Mediterranean. Now a days there is a train that connects the villages, and a modern highway. We flew into Milan and took a beautiful train trip to the beginning of the Cinque Terre. We stayed in hostels each night.

The Pyrenees Mountains in Spain and France.

We hiked the Pyrenees Mountains that started in Southern France and continued into Northern Spain. Each morning we would hike into the Pyrenees Mountains on trails. In the evening, we would go back down to the Mediterranean and stay in beautiful hotels specifically for hikers like us. We had our suitcases portaged from hotel to hotel each day of the hike. We saw olive groves that monks had planted 500 years earlier, and small rock huts that had been in use 2000 years ago. Incredible.

Forest hikes I've done in Washington State are:

Dungeness National Wildlife Refuge.

One can see the San Juan Islands and Canada from this beautiful 7-mile-long spit. The beaches are flat with hard packed sand (so they're easy to walk on). We've brought a lunch here to enjoy and then have found a hide-a-way in the huge driftwood logs to take a nap in.

Hurricane Ridge.

This is the gem of the Pacific Northwest. One can see in all directions from 4500 feet up as the views are…. simply stunning. Folks come from all over the world to see this beauty. 12 miles from Port Angeles into the Olympic Mountains.

1) **Royal Basin** hike is a 7 mile (1 way), 5000-foot elevation gain- and the wildflowers are always superb.

Some girlfriends and I backpacked this about four years ago and decided we would never backpack again…. too difficult! Yet, some folks hike up there and back in a single day. This is in the National Park.

2) A flatter hike is the **Upper Dungeness** Hike. Is about 3.5 miles one way. This is located in the National Forest.

3) Hiking **Mount Townsend** is beautiful (4 miles one way, 2900-foot elevation gain). Located in the National Park.

4) **Tubal Cain Mine and Buckhorn Lake Hike** (6 miles one way, 2000-foot elevation gain). This is also stunning, but not as stunning as Mount Townsend.

I was a forest ranger for the Olympic National Forest (not Park) a number of years ago. There are so many incredible hikes to do both in the National Forest and Park.

PLAYING GAMES (Games we like).

Scrabble is a good word game that you can play with up to six people. Have a dictionary nearby and don't allow the young digital natives use their phone to come up with exotic words.

Phase 10 is a great easy rummy card game to play with up to six people. My son and I played many games of Phase 10 while he was growing up. (My friend Jean has said that the only time I want to quit playing Phase 10 is when she's ahead!)

Uno is good if you have kids in your life six years old or so. An easy game for adults too.

Chess is good to teach your kids if they're six or so. Chess is a good critical thinking game.

Checkers is good game to play with children three years or older.

Monopoly (the board game) is also great to play with children. You add a beautiful lunch or dinner while you're playing, and it becomes a fantastic way to spend the afternoon inside when the weather is inclement.

Music in a variety of ways can easily be enjoyed. Many radio stations have old time mystery shows (like Sherlock Holmes) on the weekend that could be enjoyable for a family to listen to. We usually have classical music in the background if we're dining inside.

FOOD

As said earlier, we here in our beautiful community get together once or twice weekly to dine, drink, and play games. Lots of fun! Elaine may make her famous spinach balls, Jim sometimes brings his homemade applesauce or some home-grown vegetables, and Jerry's known for his beautiful vegetarian lasagna. Me, I make spaghetti, sometimes chicken and dumplings, and sometimes legumes with vegetables. Elaine and I do double duty for dessert; Elaine's homemade chocolate cake and ice cream are always big hits.

Sadly, America has become a land of obesity. One can walk in grocery stores, high schools, and other populated places and see that 50% of folks are obese. Not all folks are fatties, certainly, but many of us are heavier and chunkier than we should be for optimum health. One cannot be as healthy as possible if we're fat. Our culture is one that is filled with a variety of foods that we eat at all hours of the day. We eat breakfast, then sit in an office and eat donuts only before we go out for lunch-and this continues throughout the day-constantly stuffing our pie hole with more and varied stuff; and most of it not even real food. You know what I'm getting at…. how much healthier would we be if we ate foods in their natural state? Instead of potato chips, we'd eat potatoes. Instead of chicken strips, we'd buy a single piece or two of organic chicken to cook; and then enjoy the skin on that as well. Some nutritionists suggest that we only eat foods that our forefathers would've eaten 100 years ago; foods in their organic natural state. You can use the good old fashioned fast food (the kind that we would've eaten 100 years ago), a hardboiled egg (or two) and an apple for lunch put into your coat pocket as you head out the door for work (rather than a fast-food burger).

Growing organic: Alas, I am not naturally a gifted, green gardener, as point in fact I am not a gardener at all! I have to work to remember to water my vegetables and potatoes daily (I feel so guilty…). Many ladies (and fella's), though, take to gardening like a duck takes to water. I cannot recommend specific tips here, but many folks who live off grid take great delight in growing all kinds of yummy healthy food. I have planted a small orchard (apples, plums, apricots, figs), and do have a small green garden (spinach and chard). And being the Finnish peasant girl that I am, I have a large potato garden. I love potatoes. I love them baked, I love them fried, I especially love them mashed with gravy over them, scalloped, boiled, you name it, and I love potatoes. Potatoes are an inexpensive staple. If you have kids and family, potatoes may be something that you want to grow lots of. What's great about potatoes is that when you harvest them in the fall, they can last six months (or longer) in a root cellar or outside pantry. Some gardeners say that we should spend energy growing the specialty vegetables that cost more (like tomatoes or artichokes). You may want to subscribe to this theory too, and just grow the more expensive vegetables or alternatively, you may want to grow vegetables that you and your family especially like.

Chickens: Oh chickens! Link for Polish chickens: https://bit.ly/PolishChickens *

Chickens are about as much fun as a country girl can possibly have! I used to have some Polish Chickens that had the funniest Phyllis Diller kind of feathered topknot of a hat. Every time they'd run anywhere, the huge, puffy feathered hat they'd be growing would sway this way and that-too funny to watch! Most gals off grid buy their organic poultry in the spring, raise their beauties during the spring and summer, and then once a week (or more often) butcher a chicken for a Sunday dinner.

I know of a group of women who each dedicate themselves to a particular facet of growing food for their collective community of ten families; one woman raises chickens, another woman a beef, a third woman makes beer, etc. In the fall, this community of ten women will gather at the home of the gal who raised the chickens to butcher their chickens. After butchering the chickens, they each freeze their share of the chickens to eat throughout the winter. This group of women that butchers' chickens together call themselves "The Mother Pluckers". The Mother Pluckers! Hilarious! I was so happy to be told this story!

Chickens are also known for something essential to gardening and something that they have lots of: chicken poop. Yes indeed, chicken poop is super good (after a time) for a vegetable garden. Or, if your chickens can free range (the very best possible situation), they can drop their nutritional deposits around your yard so that the whole yard becomes stronger and healthier. While I'm on this thought, my mother made the very best chicken salad: here's the recipe!

MOTHER'S CHICKEN SALAD RECIPE

> 2 cups cooked chicken chopped
> ½ cup mayonnaise
> 1 stalk celery
> 1 green onion
> 1 teaspoon Dijon mustard
> ½ teaspoon salt

Mix all together and put on lovely wholewheat bread. Some folks add raisins or nuts, but I generally don't appreciate extra add on with food like this.

Various books are written about the best kinds of chickens to have for eggs and/or eating. It seems like I'm normally given young hens, so I've never bought a certain kind of chicken on my own. I've helped a few times with chicken butchering. I feel strongly (now) that we should all be familiar with the butchering process *if* we eat meat. The factory processes that are used in chicken and egg production (and that our grocery stores are selling) are inhumane. If you're over 18 years old, you know what I'm talking about. Don't let this be you.

BEANS

If you want to eat less meat (for health or for expenses), beans (commonly called legumes) are a great bet. You can buy legumes in ten-pound bags and those, with a variety of vegetables, make *incredible,* simple meals. I always have about 25 pounds of different beans in my pantry available to use at a moments' notice. We had a new couple move into the neighborhood a while back. This lovely couple came to my home bringing beautiful homemade muffins. While we enjoyed a bit of wine, and toasted to their health and well-being, I started a bean soup that would complement their muffins. I always keep fresh vegetables on hand too, simply to allow me to make a great meal. After a while, we ate this delicious homemade soup with their muffins and butter and honey. If you think about the importance of hospitality, you may want to keep this kind of food on hand. Being a gracious hostess is so *so grand*….it just takes a little planning for that spur of the moment celebratory dinners. (FYI, I also keep bottles of wine and liquor on hand as well).

Garbanzo Beans:

A terrific garbanzo bean dish can be made with sautéed tomatoes, onions, and garlic in butter. Dried garbanzo beans take about 1-1.5 hours to cook. I cook all of the water out of the tomatoes and onions while the garbanzo beans are cooking. I normally add a little salt and pepper and serve with cornbread and honey. This is a beautiful meal and so healthy.

Black Beans:

Black beans boiled for about an hour are ready to have carrots, onions, and garlic added. This is also a terrific dish to serve with homemade potato bread and butter.

Potato Bread recipe: This is a great base for cinnamon rolls too!

    2 cups mashed potatoes

    1 and ½ cups milk

    1/3 cup butter

    2 tablespoons honey

    2 teaspoons salt

2 packages of active dry yeast

½ cup warm water

2 eggs

8 cups all-purpose flour.

Peel potatoes and boil until tender, drain, and mash. Slowly stir in milk, butter, honey and salt. If necessary, heat to 110 degrees. Meanwhile, in large bowl, mix yeast with water, let stand 5 minutes. Combine potato mixture, eggs and 3 C flour. Gradually mix in 3 and ½ C more flour. Turn out on a floured board, knead until smooth and elastic, about 10 minutes, adding more flour as needed. Place dough in greased bowl, turn to grease top. Cover let rise in warm place until doubled, about 1 and ½ hours. Punch dough down, divine in thirds. Shape each portion into a smooth loaf, place in three well-greased 9 by 5-inch bread pans. Cover, let rise in warm place until almost double, about 30-40 minutes. Bake at 350 degrees for 35 to 40 minutes or until loaves are browned and sound hollow when tapped. Turn out of pans, cool on racks.

Kidney Beans:

A vegetarian minestrone can be made simply with kidney beans and garbanzo beans. Cook the beans until you can squish one between your fingers (about 1.5 hours). Add tomatoes (or a can of tomatoes), greens (spinach or chard), carrots, celery, and onions. Voila! A fabulous dinner without meat (I always add salt and pepper to taste). Some folks add hamburger, ground turkey or sausage to this, but we sometimes prefer to have our calories in our lovely fruit-in-season daiquiris (rather than the meat). Health is important to everyone who lives off grid. If one does not stay healthy, then quite often, one cannot continue to live off-grid

Foods in their natural state:

A gal I know who was a nutritionist for Stanford University gave me sage advice many years ago. She said that if a person is healthy, then they don't need to consider calories, salt, or anything else that smacks of dietary deprivation *if only* one would eat foods in their natural state. So instead of potato chips, we should eat potatoes, instead of twinkies or ding-dongs, we should eat a single small

square of good quality dark chocolate, etc. The nutritionist also said
that healthy people should be able to eat the skin on organic
chickens as well. This was a beautiful bit of information for me as
we've all been inundated with media bullshit advising us to not eat
fat and that we should drink low-fat milk, skim the fat off gravies, etc.
Most folks aren't aware that human beings *are the only* animals that
drink milk after being weaned from their mother's breast. Some folks
who do enjoy milk, may want to get their own milk cow (or goat),
and drink it raw and fresh from the animal.

Dinners and dining with the people you love: (recipes, drinks,
discussions, laughter, joy) with a local classical music radio station
on and/or playing homemade music, etc. is such a beautiful way to
enjoy an evening meal!

IV. GOAL SETTING.

Most of the time management gurus (experts) suggest that everyone have written down goals. So, think here…. if you could do, be, or have anything in the world, what would it be? And meditate on this particular fact in living well; you are currently living *exactly* the life you've planned for yourself. *You are right now living exactly the life you've planned for yourself.* You can never pass the buck and blame somebody else, as *every aspect* of your life is your responsibility. Are you happy? Healthy? Are you with people who matter to you? Do you want to spend more time with family? Less time? When I divorced years ago, I was so sad…. the husband that I was so crazy about ten years earlier was spending his time at the bar drinking with good-time buddies (and other activities as well). Try as I may, I was unable to change him (hmmm, imagine that!), so I chose the lesser of two evils (for me) which resulted in divorce. Now, years later, (after a few backward slides), I've created a stunningly beautiful life for myself and my family. Being able to take 100% responsibility for every aspect of your life is so…. so…. important. Don't let yourself blame others for *you* living the life you have…. do what it takes to get you to where you want to be. *Do what it takes to get you to where you want to be.*

So now we get to where you need to think, *really think*, about how you want your life to be. Our culture doesn't encourage critical thinking skills, yet without them, we become the robots that have permeated all aspects of our culture. Imagine yourself throwing away all of the mind programming that you've had since you were five years old. If you (as an individual) had the ability to live a certain way (that's different than how your parents thought you should live, different than how your pastor thought you should live, different than how your schoolteachers thought you should live), what would that way be? You may have an inkling *right at this exact moment* how your preferred life would look. Write that down right now. And then meditate on this for a few minutes how your preferred life would look if your *life were perfect.* Write this down as well.

If your life were perfect, how would it look five years from now? If money or time were not an issue, how would your life look? Would you *finally* be sleeping enough? Eating only organic? In school? Have a new (or better or different or part-time) job? Take a vacation? I've known folks who, after planning for and then beginning to live an intentional life, go on a six-month sailing trip with their children, and others who, after deciding to homeschool their children, have spent one year traveling the world with their children all the while learning about the places they're visiting. How would it be to have your children grow up with your values because *you're* the one schooling them? Write down everything that you *want to have*, everything that you *want to do*, and everything that you *want to be (do this for yourself first, and then do it again for your family)*.

FIVE-YEAR GOALS:

1)

2)

3)

4)

5)

6)

7)

8)

9)

10)

ONE YEAR GOALS: What do you need to do between now and next year to get closer to your five-year goals?

1)

2)

3)

4)

5)

6)

7)

8)

9)

10)

SIX MONTH GOALS: Write down what you need to do between now and six months from now to get closer to your five-year goals.

1)

2)

3)

4)

5)

6)

7)

8)

9)

10)

ONE MONTH GOALS: Write down what you need to do between now and next month to get close to your five-year goals.

1)

2)

3)

4)

5)

6)

7)

8)

9)

10)

V. CONCLUSION

You should have a clear picture of what you want in life at this point. Perhaps you've done these kinds of exercises in the past-you know that if you *don't take action* nothing will happen! There's an old saying "if you want more of what you have, keep doing what you've always done". This is a true statement! If you want to live a different life than what you have today, you must *do* your life differently! And you don't have to radically change it *today*; you can, however, make subtle changes *today* (walk every day at lunchtime rather than go out to eat, apply for a 2nd part time job to pay off debt, go to the library and check out movies there rather than paying for movie services). Prepare to downsize your life; look into having a roommate (or becoming a roommate), get rid of as many monthly payments as you can; do you really need that gym membership? How about that fancy car with the fancy car payments each month? Dave Ramsey's class on financial stewardship, Peace University, is indeed a peace learning class as it relates to finances. Would you like to have peace of mind with your finances? Go online now and sign up for Ramsey's class. It could profoundly change your life today as it has thousands of others. Also. This is super important......... If someone else is living like how you want, then it becomes salient that you *as well* can live like that; if someone else has done it, you can too!

In closing, I wish for you to take measures to live your ideal life. Be careful what you say to your friends and family; some will support you, some won't. It may be beneficial to keep close to your heart your new plans; there will be a later time that you can let your extended family and friends in on what you're doing.

Life is good. If you're healthy, your life should always be *great*, beautiful, and full of love. Become the person that you most want to be. Become the person that you've always known you could be. Make your life happen!